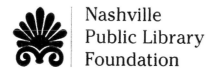

Nashville
Public Library
Foundation

In honor of

Phyllis Baker Vandewater
and
Emily Robinson Vandewater

SandCastle 3

Long Vowels

Ii

Mary Elizabeth Salzmann

ABDO
Publishing Company

Published by SandCastle™, an imprint of ABDO Publishing Company, 4940 Viking Drive, Edina, Minnesota 55435.

Printed in the United States.

Cover and Interior Photo credits: Comstock, Digital Stock, Eyewire Images, Photodisc

Library of Congress Cataloging-in-Publication Data

Salzmann, Mary Elizabeth, 1968-
    Ii / Mary Elizabeth Salzmann.
      p. cm. -- (Long vowels)
    Includes index.
    ISBN 1-57765-415-3
    1. Readers (Primary) [1. English language--Phonetics.] I. Title.

PE1119 .S23423 2000
428.1--dc21

00-033209

The SandCastle concept, content, and reading method have been reviewed and approved by a national advisory board including literacy specialists, librarians, elementary school teachers, early childhood education professionals, and parents.

Let Us Know

After reading the book, SandCastle would like you to tell us your stories about reading. What is your favorite page? Was there something hard that you needed help with? Share the ups and downs of learning to read. We want to hear from you! To get posted on the Abdo Publishing Company Web site, send us email at:

sandcastle@abdopub.com

Revised Edition 2002

About SandCastle™

Nonfiction books for the beginning reader

- Basic concepts of phonics are incorporated with integrated language methods of reading instruction. Most words are short, and phrases, letter sounds, and word sounds are repeated.

- Readability is determined by the number of words in each sentence, the number of characters in each word, and word lists based on curriculum frameworks.

- Full-color photography reinforces word meanings and concepts.

- "Words I Can Read" list at the end of each book teaches basic elements of grammar, helps the reader recognize the words in the text, and builds vocabulary.

- Reading levels are indicated by the number of flags on the castle.

Look for more SandCastle books in these three reading levels:

Level 1
(one flag)

Level 2
(two flags)

Level 3
(three flags)

Grades Pre-K to K
5 or fewer words per page

Grades K to 1
5 to 10 words per page

Grades 1 to 2
10 to 15 words per page

Ii

I know fun ways to have
a fine time.

What do you like to do?

Ira likes to swing on his tire swing.

He got it when he was five.

Irene likes to practice the violin outside.

She has a recital on Friday.

Isis likes to slide.

She has done it nine times.

Isaac likes to go on long hikes.

He can hike for many miles.

Ivy likes to ride her bike.

She rides down the drive.

Ivan likes to climb.

He is trying to climb this white sign.

We like to fly our kite very high.

It has blue and yellow stripes.

Ivo likes to ice-skate.

What color are his ice skates?

(white)

Words I Can Read

Nouns

A noun is a person, place, or thing

bike (BIKE) p. 15
color (KUHL ur) p. 21
drive (DRIVE) p. 15
hikes (HIKESS) p. 13
ice skates (EYESS
  SKAYTSS) p. 21
kite (KITE) p. 19

miles (MILEZ) p. 13
recital (ri-SYE-tuhl) p. 9
sign (SINE) p. 17
stripes (STRIPESS)
  p. 19
time (TIME) p. 5
times (TIMEZ) p. 11

tire swing
  (TIRE SWING) p. 7
violin (vye-uh-LIN) p. 9
ways (WAYZ) p. 5
white (WITE) p. 21

Proper Nouns

A proper noun is the name of a person, place, or thing

Friday (FRYE-day) p. 9
Ira (EYE-ruh) p. 7
Irene (eye-REEN) p. 9

Isaac (EYE-zik) p. 13
Isis (EYE-siss) p. 11
Ivan (EYE-vuhn) p. 17

Ivo (EYE-voh) p. 21
Ivy (EYE-vee) p. 15

Pronouns

A pronoun is a word that replaces a noun

he (HEE) pp. 7, 13, 17
I (EYE) p. 5
it (IT) pp. 7, 11, 19

she (SHEE) pp. 9, 11, 15
we (WEE) p. 19
what (WUHT) pp. 5, 21

you (YOO) p. 5

Verbs

A verb is an action or being word

are (AR) p. 21
can (KAN) p. 13
climb (KLIME) p. 17
do (DOO) p. 5
done (DUHN) p. 11
fly (FLYE) p. 19
go (GOH) p. 13
got (GOT) p. 7
has (HAZ) pp. 9, 11, 19

have (HAV) p. 5
hike (HIKE) p. 13
ice-skate (EYESS-
   skayt) p. 21
is (IZ) p. 17
know (NOH) p. 5
like (LIKE) pp. 5, 19
likes (LIKESS) pp. 7, 9,
   11, 13, 15, 17, 21

practice (PRAK-tiss)
   p. 9
ride (RIDE) p. 15
rides (RIDEZ) p. 15
slide (SLIDE) p. 11
swing (SWING) p. 7
trying (TRYE-ing) p. 17
was (WUHZ) p. 7

Adjectives

An adjective describes something

blue (BLOO) p. 19
fine (FINE) p. 5
five (FIVE) p. 7
fun (FUHN) p. 5
her (HUR) p. 15

high (HYE) p. 19
his (HIZ) pp. 7, 21
long (LAWNG) p. 13
many (MEN-ee) p. 13
nine (NINE) p. 11

our (AR) p. 19
this (THISS) p. 17
white (WITE) p. 17
yellow (YEL-oh) p. 19

Adverbs

An adverb tells how, when, or where
something happens

outside (out-SIDE) p. 9   very (VER-ee) p. 19

23

Glossary

hike – a long walk, usually in the country.

ice skates – boots with blades on the bottom to help you glide on ice.

recital – a short musical performance by a single person.

violin – a musical instrument with four stings that is played with a bow.

More Iī Words

bite	kind	rise
child	life	smile
dime	minus	tiger
find	night	umpire
hi	pile	vine
idea	quite	write